BRITAIN IN PICTURES
THE BRITISH PEOPLE IN PICTURES

ENGLISH
POPULAR AND TRADITIONAL ART

GENERAL EDITOR
W. J. TURNER

The Editor is most grateful to all those who have
so kindly helped in the selection of illustrations
especially to officials of the various public
Museums Libraries and Galleries and
to all others who have generously
allowed pictures and MSS
to be reproduced

ENGLISH POPULAR
AND TRADITIONAL ART

ENID MARX
MARGARET LAMBERT

*WITH
8 PLATES IN COLOUR
AND
30 ILLUSTRATIONS IN
BLACK & WHITE*

COLLINS · 14 ST. JAMES'S PLACE · LONDON
MCMXLVI

PRODUCED BY
ADPRINT LIMITED LONDON

PRINTED IN GREAT BRITAIN
BY JARROLD AND SONS LTD NORWICH
ON MELLOTEX BOOK PAPER MADE
BY TULLIS RUSSELL AND CO LTD MARKINCH SCOTLAND

LIST OF ILLUSTRATIONS

PLATES IN COLOUR

BLACK AND WHITE ILLUSTRATIONS

Illustrations on pp. 7, 11, 19, 33, 39, 40, 41, 46, 47 and 48 are reproduced by permission of Mrs. Nicholl, who most generously made her collection available to us

CUT-OUT PAPER VALENTINE

INTRODUCTION

POPULAR and traditional art, in the sense here intended, is hard to define though easy enough to recognise when seen. It is the art which ordinary people have, from time immemorial, introduced into their everyday lives, sometimes making it themselves, at others imposing their own tastes on the products of the craftsman or the machine, in contrast to the more sophisticated art made by specialists for wealthy patrons. Its very lack of sophistication makes popular art one of the most revealing expressions of national characteristics. Because it is more conspicuous amongst simple non-industrial societies, many people have supposed that its only genuine form is peasant or folk art. This book is an attempt to show that in England too, although peasants may no longer exist, we have a long and living tradition of popular art, which not only survived the industrial revolution, but in some cases, such as fair-ground decoration (or, to take an earlier example, printing) even drew new inspiration from the potentialities of the machine. Whatever the causes for the present very noticeable decline in aesthetic standards, they certainly seem to go far deeper than the generally accepted explanation that machinery and mass production destroy individual taste. A curious fact which seems to emerge from this brief

7

survey is that the last great impetus to popular art came from the Romantic Movement in the early years of the nineteenth century; there has been nothing comparable since.

It is not, of course, possible in so small a compass to cover the whole field, and selection has had to be most arbitrary. We have tried to give some idea of the many forms, however simple, in which English popular art has manifested itself and to show its distinctive qualities: forthrightness, gaiety, delight in bright colours and sense of well-balanced design. For convenience and brevity the examples have been roughly grouped by the materials used and types of decoration.

PAPER AND PRINTING

STREET literature, the literature of the masses, provides some of the most interesting forms of popular art in England. It owes its existence to cheap printing, but printing, once discovered, was surprisingly quickly adapted to the popular traditions. The ordinary purveyor of litera-ture to the countryside, the itinerant ballad singer, who often combined this with the role of miscellaneous pedlar, could now sell printed copies of his songs as well as singing them, thereby enhancing their value for his simple-minded audience.

Ballads and broadsides, being intended for a not very literate public, needed a strong pictorial appeal. A large woodcut would be printed at the head of a long strip of paper, the length varying according to the amount of matter (often topical verses set to traditional tunes) to be printed under-neath. These broadside woodcuts, though often coarsely cut, have in their simplicity, directness and freedom, much of the attraction of primitive paintings; they are done in the same spirit as the grotesqueries and humours of misereres or gargoyles in Gothic churches. Ordinary people have always delighted in the marvellous, the dramatic and horrific. Literal pictorial representation of marvels entailed a glorious juxtaposition of incongruous objects, often producing a much more fantastic effect than the deliberate surrealism of modern painters.

Before dying out in the mid-nineteenth century, broadsides declined in the social scale, circulating mainly amongst the rougher and more brutal sections of society. The ballad-sellers became the Flying Stationers or Running Patterers like Silas Wegg in *Our Mutual Friend*. Until 1839, when this was forbidden on account of the din, they would run through the streets of London blowing a horn and crying excerpts from the latest "bloody battle" or "horrible murder," done into broadside doggerel. When sensations were scarce, an old one would be palmed off as new; hence the title "Catchpenny."

8

PEDLAR DOLL SHOWING MISCELLANEOUS WARES
Early nineteenth century
Collection Mrs. Nicholl

TINSELLED ENGRAVINGS USED AS PICTURES IN COTTAGES
Early nineteenth century
Collection Mrs. Nicholl

FRONTISPIECE FROM PARK'S *NEW EGYPTIAN DREAM BOOK*
Hand-coloured engraving of the early nineteenth century
Collection Mrs. Nicholl

Murder, then as now, was a great attraction. Public executions stimulated a brisk trade in the "Gallows Literature" type of broadside; especially popular were "Last Confessions," in doggerel verse with a high moral tone and written, so the Patterer pretended, "in the condemned cell, with the condemned pen, ink and paper." They were given stock portraits, used over and over again, the wood blocks being recut from time to time from earlier originals. But this lack of factual realism never seems to have worried the broadside public; indeed, though dictated by economy, it suited an audience which, being only partly literate, could more easily recognise stock characters like those of pantomime or melodrama. The conception of realism in art is really quite modern. Orlando Hodgson, for instance, produced an illustration of the Greenacre crime with such brilliant and unnaturalistic colour combinations that the gruesomeness of individual details disappears in the theatricality and artificiality of the whole. The result is superb.

Though sensationalism bulked large, the Running Stationer's stock, even towards the end of his existence, was by no means confined to it. Dialogues of all kinds, humorous, elevating, satirical; political squibs, moral tracts, songs "three yards a penny," comic, serious, religious, love songs, drinking songs, patriotic ballads, all embellished with cuts, some most inappropriate, were printed in great variety. One of the last historic events to be recorded in broadside chronicles was Victoria's marriage to Albert in 1840. Jemmy Catnatch and Johnny Pitts, the two rival printers of the Seven Dials district, produced sentiments to suit all tastes; in some Albert was represented as a Prince Charming, in others as a German sausage merchant. In wartime the ballad-monger was the great patriotic historian.

News purveyor, entertainer, scandal-monger, patriot, he was also, oddly enough, a great moralist. We find broadsides, all through their career, dwelling on the vanities of this world and the imminence of death. Sometimes old verses are given contemporary pictures, as in "Death and Mortality" illustrated here.

The simplicity and directness of the broadside woodcuts made them extremely effective propaganda. George Cruikshank, for instance, in his campaign to abolish the death penalty for forgery, adopts the broadside style with remarkably dramatic effect.

Complementary to the broadsides, though originating somewhat later, often produced by the same printers and covering many of the same topics, were the Chapbooks, called after the Chapman who sold them. They were slim, small, paper-covered volumes, easy to fit into a pedlar's pack. Small woodcuts usually ornamented their cover or frontispiece and were interspersed in the text, as pictures and swags. These little cuts constitute the special charm of the chapbooks; they have the *naïveté*, directness and fantasy of ballad and broadside decorations, but being on a smaller scale, display more delicacy. The paper covers of chapbooks deserve special

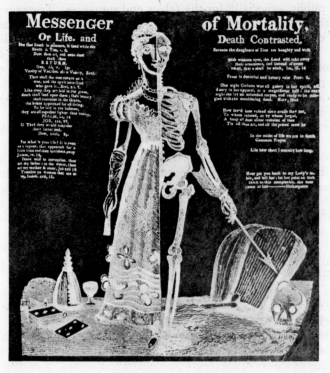

BROADSIDE, C. 1830

mention; they were often gaily coloured (yellow was a favourite ground) with, sometimes, little stuck-on labels for the titles, surrounded with pretty little type ornaments and perhaps a woodcut, hand-coloured. Decorated papers also were used with great effect.

Chapbooks flourished exceedingly from the middle of the seventeenth century onwards. Ranging in price from sixpence to a penny or less, they cover an immense variety of topics. John Ashton, the nineteenth-century antiquarian, made a rough classification, which runs: "Religious, Diabolical, Supernatural, Superstitious, Romantic, Humorous, Legendary, Historical, Biographical and Criminal." The contents can rarely claim any literary merit. The stories, some based on real events, others on old medieval romances, others again crude pirated versions of popular books, such as *Gulliver's Travels*, are generally so hacked about and compressed that at times they hardly make sense. The chapbooks' attraction lies mainly in their illustrations.

Chapbooks specially for children were a late development, as were all children's books not primarily designed as an adjunct to lessons or for moral instruction. Nevertheless, children must have formed a large part of the

10

chapbook public, especially for the fables and romances; Tristram Shandy's Uncle Toby bought them for his schoolfellows. When at last a real publisher of books for children appeared—John Newbery, publisher and friend of Johnson, Goldsmith and Smollett—he followed the chapbook tradition of small pictures and miniature size, with gay covers of Dutch embossed papers, but with the text directly written for children. Even the great Bewick kept to the old chapbook style in his wood engravings for the children's books published, some years after Newbery, by Saint of Newcastle—for instance the delightful *New Lottery Book of Birds and Beasts* (1771).

Chapbooks were frowned on by moralists as putting fanciful ideas into children's heads. Mr. Harvey Darton, the great authority, points out in his *Children's Books in England*, that the battle of the Puritans, the struggle between Penny Merriments and Penny Godlinesses, raged in the chapbook world as elsewhere. Nevertheless, apart from their intrinsic charm, chapbooks made two immortal contributions to our nursery archives; to them alone is due the survival of the Fairy Tale and Nursery Rhyme, which would else have disappeared with the oral traditions which first put them into circulation as children's tales.

Early in the nineteenth century appeared what its publishers called the Juvenile Drama, better known perhaps as the Toy Theatre, or "Penny Plain and Twopence Coloured."

If you bought a Juvenile Drama complete, as you still could till 1944, it would consist of a little book of words, stage directions and instructions; a given number of sheets of scenery—backcloths and wings; a smaller number

GEORGE CRUIKSHANK'S BROADSIDE AGAINST THE DEATH PENALTY FOR FORGERY

of sheets of characters, and, in the case of a pantomime, a sheet or two of tricks. These sheets would be pictures in outline, either plain for colouring yourself, or, for an extra penny, hand-coloured by professionals with a verve and brilliance the amateur could scarcely hope to emulate. These sheets, to be mounted on cardboard and cut out according to directions, were meant for use on the little wooden frame stages which, complete with gaily coloured proscenium, a real drop curtain and tin holders for footlights, could be bought for about a pound. The stage once set, the characters (in different attitudes according to the action of the plot) were slid on and off from the wings as directed in the book of words. Pantomime "trick" changes were done by dropping little flaps cut in the scenery. For moments of high drama, fireworks might be used; "red fire to burn" is the usual stage direction for the frequent conflagrations required by the plots. Mr. A. E. Wilson, in his fascinating book *Penny Plain and Twopence Coloured*, suggests that the idea of the cut-out model theatre may have come from abroad. The Peepshow was a well-known institution at fairs and the toy theatre is in the same tradition as the peepshow. But whatever its origin, the Juvenile Drama, once arrived, had a great success. The plays and pantomimes presented were taken from the contemporary stage. The characters, especially in the early days, were often faithful portraits of famous players. Stage fronts are, as like as not, taken from well-known theatres. Street scenes, too, are often from life; one of Pollock's shows his own shop. Apart from their intrinsic charm, these little theatres preserve a wonderfully vivid record of the early nineteenth-century stage, even down to the exaggerated gestures, the strut and swagger of the romantic type of acting then fashionable.

This stage lent itself exceptionally well to adaptation for the toy theatre. In literary merit it has probably never been so bad, but action and magnificent spectacle made up for stereotyped characters and artificial plots. The Gothic Revival had merged into the full tide of the Romantic Movement; the stage, like literature, painting and even architecture, was luxuriating in a riot of medieval, Oriental, or otherwise exotic splendour. To meet the demand for what we should now call "actuality," recent events such as the battles of Waterloo and Trafalgar, even the burning of Moscow, were turned into stage and toy theatre dramas, where they provided scope for *tours de force* in scenic display. The first hints of a decline in the toy theatre's popularity coincide with the change that came over the English theatre as a reaction set in towards naturalism and the comedy of manners, dependent for its effect on dialogue rather than on display.

Some publishers dealt only in Juvenile Drama, but the great majority also went in for much else in the cheaper forms of literature; children's books, almanacs, books of fate in the chapbook tradition, coloured engravings and cartoons, Valentines and such-like things. In *Vanity Fair*, Thackeray refers to "West's famous characters," and William West was

CHILD'S INSCRIBED WRITING SHEET

certainly a most prolific producer; Mr. Wilson has found as many as a hundred and seven plays published by him, ~~which gives~~ some idea of the immense vogue the toy theatre enjoyed; West's nautical dramas are some of his most superb and dramatic productions. Another prolific toy theatre sheet publisher was Skelt, from whom Robert Louis Stevenson coined the descriptive word "Skeltery" to epitomise this miniature world of romance. Webb and Pollock (late Reddington) were still carrying on their family businesses until a few years ago, though of course only reissuing old plays.

In their style of drawing and dramatic use of colour, the toy theatre sheets do not break new ground. They follow the same tradition as the coloured engravings, hung on many a cottage wall, or used as illustrations to the various types of cheap paper-covered booklets and pamphlets issued

13

for popular amusement by the same publishers. The frontispiece to the Book of Fate here illustrated, and published by Park, one of the best of the toy theatre publishers, is in the same style of draughtsmanship and colour range.

Many other examples could be cited, such as some of the children's books and games, the coloured borders to their writing sheets, the cheaper type of gardening papers just coming into vogue with their pictures of gaily splashed and speckled "florist's flowers."

The means available for producing these effects were of the simplest; flat washes of water colour on outline drawings, with the minimum of line shading. The basic colours used were usually limited to four—gamboge, carmine, prussian blue and black. Skilful mixing and graduations produced luscious browns, purples, greens, pinks. It is remarkable how sheets over a century old retain their brilliance. Much of the secret seems to lie in the excellent quality of the pigments used and in the imaginative skill shown in juxtaposing one colour with another to set each off to best advantage.

The draughtsmanship too is often of a high order. Some of the earlier publishers, notably West, Jamieson, and Hodgson, used well-known artists. West at one time even employed William Blake. Nevertheless, so strong was the convention, that artists of the most marked individuality seem to fit into it quite comfortably. Partly this is due to the very simple reproductive process used; the artist's sketches were engraved, and the colour hand-painted by teams of children, or perhaps the members of a family. For later productions stencils came in. Stencilling does not give the same tone gradations as direct painting, but has its own attractions in the firmer outline and greater effect of freedom.

If we take a well-known play, such as the melodrama *The Miller and his Men,* and compare the versions produced by the different publishers from the same original, we can easily distinguish one from the other in individualities of style and selection; which shows that the toy theatre artists displayed plenty of initiative and originality. Much of the charm of their work lies in the way the prevailing Romanticism, the passion for things rich and strange, has been interpreted into homely English terms, thereby producing an extraordinary mixture of the real and the fantastic. Just as, half a century later, the village painter, the Douanier Rousseau, was to base his tigers on the ordinary village cat, so the toy theatre artists made up their tropical forests from everyday English vegetation but of a supernatural luxuriance. Robert Louis Stevenson was fascinated by the extreme boskiness of the Skeltonian forests, the excessive gnarledness possible to a plain English oak. The intricately pinnacled castles, washed by rivers of an inky blue, obviously derive from the same originals as the castles still painted on canal barges to-day. Styles of architecture, or costume, Egyptian, Oriental, Central European, are jumbled together in exuberant confusion. The heights of fantasy are reached in the pantomimes. Tradition demands

14

N.27   MISS. VINCENT as NEPTUNE in FLYING DUTCHMAN.

PICTURE FOR TINSELLING PUBLISHED BY PARK

that Harlequin with his bat, or Clown with the poker, shall turn everyday objects into something unexpected. Toy theatre tricks follow the pantomime tradition, where part of the fun lies in arbitrarily altering the size of ordinary objects; an egg turns into a huge hen bigger than the clown and so on. Tricks were, of course, meant to be cut out, but the sheets as printed, with their juxtaposition of incongruous objects, drawn to different scales and at different angles to fit the paper, give an effect of fantastic inconsequence which would be hard to achieve deliberately.

Closely akin to the Juvenile Drama are the tinsel pictures which reached their heyday about the 1830's. All toy theatre publishers also published these large engravings of celebrities, mostly theatrical but also including royal personages or popular heroes.

Decorating prints with bits of silk, satin or coloured paper was a popular amusement years before it occurred to the theatrical publishers that coloured metal foil, embossed and with a paper backing, would be effective. Tinsel ornaments in immense variety were soon produced and sold in packets for a few pence. These stamped-out tinsels included everything, from stars,

15

dots, spangles, to helmets, breastplates, plumes, even swords, daggers and pistols.

The typical tinsel picture represents the subject in heroic stance; behind him in much smaller scale is a landscape, whilst an explosive sky enhances the general effect. Some of the most attractive prints represent the hero on horseback. Heroines seldom appear: their costumes offer less scope for decoration. Most magnificent of all are the stage villains, stamping and scowling, slung about with an armoury of weapons. Some of the effects achieved with, for instance, Mephistopheles or the Ghost from *Hamlet* are superbly horrific.

Besides these big character portraits, the publishers issued smaller pictures, "fours," "sixes," or even "eights" to a sheet, which could be cut out and decorated separately, and background scenes were sold separately for mounting.

Like the Juvenile Theatres, the success of the tinsel picture depended on the vogue for romantic, unrealistic acting of the barnstorming type. With the vogue for realism and the rise of cheap colour reproductions it lost its appeal.

Not all tinsel pictures are portraits; hand-coloured engravings of highly dramatic scenes, decorated with tinsel dots and stars, may still sometimes be found hanging upon cottage walls. Indeed, any subject seems suitable for tinselling, provided it is sufficiently sensational to lend itself to the brilliancy of coloured foil.

Another form of decorated picture is the Valentine, which was once used by all classes. The idea of a Valentine made by embellishing a set of verses with a picture seems to have arrived at the end of the eighteenth century. At first such Valentines were entirely amateur; verses are composed and arranged to form patterns, and are decorated with pictures, paper cut-outs or stuck-on bits of silk or satin.

The printers soon began to take a hand. They published Valentine Writers like Letter Writers for those who could not versify themselves. Machine-made lace and embossed papers made delightful frames and borders. The hand-painted pictures forming the centres were often posies of flowers, especially the striped and speckled "florist's flowers" surrounded by an appropriate motto. Paper cut-outs in the form perhaps of hearts or true-love knots, would be likewise mounted; sometimes, with admirable skill, the inscriptions too would be cut out of paper in a single piece. Devices for pulling up one picture to show another underneath, or perhaps for opening out or sliding off the top picture, became more and more ingenious; such tricks suggested hidden sentiments which are a great part of the Valentine's attraction.

Besides supplying the accessories for making your own Valentines, printers and publishers also sold them complete. Printed Valentines included all sorts of punning effects—matrimonial ladders, cupid thermometers, pairs of gloves cut out, and adaptations of documentary forms, I.O.U.s, wills,

TOY THEATRE SHEETS

Final Tableau from *The Silver Palace*, published by B. Pollock
&
Scene from *Timour the Tartar*, published by J. Redington

NINETEENTH CENTURY CHRISTMAS CARDS
Page from an old scrapbook

VALENTINE: HAND-COLOURED LITHOGRAPH, 1845

licences, and bank notes; so realistic was a representation of a £5 Bank of Love note that it provoked action by the authorities for fear it might help forgers.

Some of the most attractive are the trade Valentines, hand-coloured engravings representing the different occupations and trades, in full costume and with suitably apt verses; there are the Chymist, the Barmaid, the Hatter, the Draper, the Pastry Cook, the Housemaid, and so on, one to fit almost any recipient.

In glaring contrast to the sentimental Valentines are the comic ones, which in crudity and brutality remind us of another aspect of English life prevalent a century ago. They consist of caricatures of different types with appropriately insulting rhymes underneath. A favourite comic transformation showed a drawing of a man or woman with a flap, which when folded back, showed the same subject minus hair and teeth. Yet in spite of their

17

crudity one cannot but recognise certain qualities of draughtsmanship and colour, sadly lacking in the modern revival of either comic or sentimental Valentines.

It may be that this ridicule led to the decline of the Valentine. But it seems more likely that they were ousted by the increasing popularity of the Christmas card.

This, as we know it to-day, is just on a hundred years old. Starting as the whim of a few well-known literary figures, who commissioned artists to design them Christmas greetings cards, the idea was promptly taken up by printers and publishers, who saw in it a much more profitable, because universal, market than the Valentine. By the 1860's, the spate of Christmas cards had begun, and they were probably at their best in the last quarter of the nineteenth century. Coming later, they miss much of the simplicity and directness which makes the aesthetic appeal of the Valentine; they are more mechanical and stereotyped, nevertheless they have a luscious exuberance not without attraction. Many of their subjects, suitably modified, are on the same principles as those of the Valentines—sentimental, floral or domestic themes, puns, adaptation of documentary forms, and so on. In variety and ingenuity, as well as in skilful use of the machine, Christmas cards probably reached their zenith in the last quarter of the nineteenth century, which is the date of those here illustrated.

"The paper cut-out, shadow profile, or silhouette, flourished most successfully in England," says Mrs. Nevill Jackson in her enchanting book *Silhouette*: this technique is, she suggests, by its sobriety and restraint, particularly suited to English taste. These shadow portraits filled the need for cheap likenesses before the invention of photography.

Cutting paper to get decorative shadowed effects is a development of missal painting. Paper was cut to look like lace, or letters of initials, or sometimes whole sentences were cut out, leaving the letters solid, in a technique which is somewhere between needlework and carving. Whilst paper was expensive, cut-paper work was mainly confined to the wealthier classes or professionals (for instance, Mrs. Delaney's exquisite flower pictures) but, in the early nineteenth century, it became cheap and accessible to all.

Cut-paper ornamentation was ideal for Valentines, and was also much used for decorating texts and mottoes, as samplers were used in needlework. From hand-made to machine-made lace-papers was a natural step, and some of the early Victorian machine-cut papers are extremely attractive.

In spite of the competition of photography, such is the fascination of the portrait silhouette that it has survived until to-day, and practitioners may still be found at seaside and other pleasure resorts. Cutting lace-paper patterns is still done by street performers to entertain queues.

Akin to cut-paper ornamentation is "pin-prick" decoration, which was also a very popular process. Combined as it usually is with a certain amount of water-colour painting, it produces extremely attractive results.

PIN-PRICK PICTURE

It depends for its effects on the contrasts between light and shade. By varying the size of the holes, and by pricking now from one side of the paper, now from the other, you can get several different textures and thus build up the pattern or picture.

In England, pin-prick decoration seems to have been first used in religious houses for decorating votive pictures and is, like cut-out silhouettes, a development of the decorated missal. But by the end of the eighteenth century it had become widely popular. The Young Ladies' Annuals which had a great vogue in the 1820's and '30's often gave instructions and suggestions for pin-prick patterns

Cut and rolled or twisted paper is another extremely effective method of paper ornament, especially for heraldic motives; it is, of course, more skilled than the ordinary pin-prick or cut-out technique.

Penmanship is yet another form of decorating paper. The various schools of English calligraphy are outside our scope and may be studied in Sir Ambrose Heal's *The English Writing Masters*. Britain's wide commercial interests naturally gave handwriting special importance. Children were encouraged to write on writing sheets, with printed hand-coloured borders, on the same principle as decorated samplers. Calligraphic styles and ornamentation were reproduced by the printers in, for instance, engraved trade cards, watch verge papers, and the like, with extremely decorative effects.

BROWN EARTHENWARE MERMAID FLASK
Early nineteenth century

POTTERY AND GLASS

SLIPWARE is one of the simplest forms of decorated pottery. The basic technique consists in taking a different coloured clay from the body of the ware, mixing it with water to a cream, and then applying it as a "slip," either all over the body or in patches to form a pattern. There are, of course, many possible variations in the way slip can be applied.

Thomas Toft and his fellows, working in the seventeenth and eighteenth centuries, represent a high-water mark in English slipware and their work is well known. What is perhaps less generally recognised is the high standard of decoration achieved by country potters, many anonymous, in most parts of England, and still sometimes to be found in remoter rural areas. They did most of their work for purely utilitarian local needs, but made special pieces on occasions (harvests, weddings, christenings or to commemorate some event), which have stood a better chance of survival. Each district tends to have its own variations in pattern and shape and its favourite method of decoration.

Typical of such small local potteries are the little group which flourished in North Devon, on the Fremington claybed, lying between Barnstaple and

Bideford. Best known of these North Devon potters are the Fishley family, established since at least the eighteenth century, and still making decorated wares in the traditional local styles until quite recently. In North Devon, as at Donyat in Somerset and on many Welsh harvest jugs, the prevalent form of decoration is a coating of slip, scratched and cut away to show the darker ground. A written inscription, enclosed in a panel, often forms part of the decorative scheme.

The pieces illustrated from North Devon are inscribed and dated at the end of the eighteenth century. They are covered with a favourite lead glaze, a rich greenish yellow, which makes the body show up as an ochreous brown and the white slip as honey-coloured. The ornamental heads on the left-hand jug are reminiscent of ships' figure-heads. Besides the usual agricultural motives, nautical ones, ships, mariner's compasses, even mermaids, are favourite subjects, as indeed might be expected in a seafaring country. Local marvels sometimes got special pictures; for instance the birth of twins joined together is commemorated in a dish, bearing their portrait and dated 1680, made at Donyat in Somerset, and now in the Taunton Museum. This is just the sort of event that the broadside writers delighted to record.

Curiously enough, although each district has its local peculiarities of shape and decoration, the sentiments described on these slipware pieces show little

21

originality. We find the same rustic apophthegms, often in the same words, all over the country. The inscriptions on the jugs illustrated run:

> "He that by the plough must thrive
> Himself must either hold or drive."

And on the right-hand Bideford harvest pitcher:

> "Harvest is come all by itself
> Now in macking of your barley mow
> When men do labour hard and sweat
> Good ale is better for their meat
> Bideford 28 April 1775."

One inscription contains a sort of potter's creed:

> "When I was in my native place
> I was a lump of clay
> And digged was from out the earth
> And brought from thence away.
> But now I am a jug become
> By potters art and skill
> And now your servant am become
> And carry ale I will."

By contrast, each district seems to have had its own set of names for the various utensils. In North Devon, for instance, the pilchard pots shipped to Cornish fishermen were, running from large to small, known as "great crocks," "buzzards" and "gallons." Ordinary red pitchers ran as "long toms," "forty tales," "gullymouths," "pinchgutts," "sixties" and "pennyjugs."

Until quite recently, that is, until the interest of dealers and collectors introduced artificial values, nearly every cottage or farmhouse mantelshelf was decorated with a row of brightly coloured earthenware chimney ornaments or "image toys" as their makers described them. Such ornaments have been the valued family possessions of many generations of country folk, and reflect, in their immense variety of forms, the taste, interests, habits, even the views, of everyday British people. In small country towns, too, it was quite common for such figures to be used for shop window display, especially in dairies, where the produce was liable to spoil in the sun.

Most of these so-called "Staffordshire" figures (in earthenware or stoneware) still to be seen in country cottages date from the late eighteenth and early nineteenth centuries; few earlier ones have survived outside the great collections.

Early stoneware saltglaze figures are now, alas, extremely rare; produced principally in Staffordshire, they are some of the most delightful works of

STAFFORDSHIRE SALTGLAZE STONEWARE FIGURES
Late eighteenth century

English potters, with a directness and humour in the best traditions of popular art. Such are the famous "Pew Groups," where two figures are shown seated on a pew, sometimes a pair of awkward young lovers, sometimes an elderly ogling couple; the groups are white but with details skilfully and wittily picked out in brown clay. Then there are the well-known owl and bear jugs, white picked out in brown, with heads that lift off to form cups. Another effective early method was the so-called "agate ware," made from layers of different coloured clays to give a streaky effect. The discovery of porcelain, however, caused the Staffordshire potters to neglect their saltglaze figures in favour of this more sophisticated material.

Earthenware figures, also made mainly in Staffordshire, held their own against the attractions of porcelain. Earthenware being the coarser and cheaper material became the "poor man's porcelain"; this humbler market naturally influenced the style of modelling, making it less sophisticated Not that porcelain models did not influence earthenware; the grave dogs, with gilt chains, that sit sentinelwise on so many cottage mantelpieces have obviously been derived at few removes from the Meissen porcelain pugs. In the process they have turned into something with a more direct and robust appeal; even with a touch of humour.

23

In looking at some of the early (Astbury Whieldon type) figures, it is curious to notice how different forms seem to get repeated in different countries and even in widely separated epochs. In the little horseman figures the stance of the horses, with their long span, is strongly reminiscent of Chinese and even African art.

All earthenware figures were not necessarily equally simple. On the contrary, some of the later figures, produced for instance by the famous Wood family, are as sophisticated as the porcelain of Chelsea or Bow, and obviously influenced by fashionable foreign models. In their genre they are very successful, but their appeal is different. The elder Ralph Wood is, however, reputed to have modelled the first of a figure which most people think of as being essentially English popular art—the Toby Jug. Variants of the Toby Philpot motive have continued right down to the present day. It is, therefore, all the more odd to find that Ralph Wood most probably derived the idea from a French model and also that the character of Toby Philpot comes from Italy, being derived from the famous mid-eighteenth-century drinking song, "the Brown Bottel," adapted from the Latin verses of an Italian author. Illustrated engravings of the song circulated all over England and thus laid the foundation of a long career.

Independently of famous firms of potters, a host of lesser ones, some known, some unknown to us to-day, carried on the production of "image toys" in the old popular tradition. Plaster moulds and enamel painting both helped to cheapen production. These wares were peddled by chapmen, or sometimes by the potter himself. A drawing by Rowlandson shows the image seller with his tray of images arriving in a country town. Mr. G. Woolliscroft Rhead in *The Earthenware Collector* gives many details of how these potters worked and he recalls an old legend current in the Potteries that one of these made the teats of his cows and the Duke of Wellington's nose from the same mould.

STAFFORDSHIRE SALTGLAZE STONEWARE
Bear-jug of the late eighteenth century

It might have been expected that the industrial revolution would have killed off what is after all a very individual art.

GLASS ROLLING-PIN—A SAILOR'S LOVE TOKEN
By courtesy of the Director of the Victoria & Albert Museum

SILVERED GLASS VASES AS USED FOR FAIRGROUND PRIZES

STAFFORDSHIRE FIGURES AND HEN EGG-DISH FROM A DEVON DAIRY WINDOW
By courtesy of the Topsham Dairy

SUNDERLAND LUSTRE MOTTO PLATE—THE ANTI-CORN-LAW CAMPAIGN, C. 1840

SUNDERLAND LUSTRE TEXT PLAQUE
From water colour sketches by Enid Marx

But at first just the contrary seems to have happened. Round about the 1830's and '40's there developed a new style of these figures, with plenty of vitality and robustness, though very simply modelled and obviously produced in large quantities. These are the "Staffordshire figures" most commonly seen about to-day. They are sometimes only fully modelled in front and of a rather flattened shape; the painting, in bright enamel on a white ground, is also often confined to the front only. But this economy in no way detracts from their charm. These figures continued to be made until late into the nineteenth century; their subsequent development falls off : indeed one can watch them deteriorate into the vulgarity of so much cheap gift pottery of to-day.

The subjects represented by these little "image toys" cover the whole range of popular interests and tastes. This is well shown by the Willett collection now in the Brighton Museum which has been assembled, not by names and dates, but by topics. Soldiers and sailors make a frequent appearance; "The Neglected Tar" is a reminder of demobilisation troubles after the Napoleonic Wars. Then there are figures in national costumes; kilted Highlanders; a Welsh couple, the lady in steeple hat, reflecting the beginnings of interest in romantic nationalism.

Amongst popular heroes and famous personages, royalty ranks high. Here we can watch the change in popular feelings towards the throne.

During George IV's reign, Queen Caroline and the King's opponents seem to have captured public sympathy; Princess Charlotte, the Heir Apparent who died young, is also frequently portrayed. William IV is chiefly associated with the Reform Bill. But with the accession of the young Queen Victoria, the domestic virtues come into their own. We can feel the popular upsurge of loyalty and affection, as shown in the lovingly modelled figures of Victoria and her Consort, their court robes giving scope for vivid sweeps of blue and red picked out in gold. Portraits of Wellington and Nelson are frequent, as one would expect. The prevailing sentiment is a robust patriotism. Strange to modern minds is the demand for figures of Napoleon, who is sympathetically presented wearing an expression of romantic melancholy. This is not the age of the illustrated press; portraits did not need to be lifelike. Wellington could at a pinch do service for Nelson. Stranger still is the fact vouched for by Mr. G. W. Rhead that, on occasion, even Wellington and Napoleon were interchangeable. Sympathies with the struggle for democracy in Europe are reflected by the inclusion of foreign patriots, for instance Garibaldi whose red shirt makes a fine show. Political passions are also recorded. From Sir Francis Burdett, Radical M.P. for Westminster, to Mr. Gladstone, popular sympathies ran mainly with the reformers. Indeed we can follow in pottery all the big political struggles of the nineteenth century—Reform Bill, Corn Laws, even Ireland.

Rather surprisingly Crime, which figures so largely in Street Literature, also finds a place in the far more durable form of pottery. An idyllic white cottage with roses growing up the walls is inscribed "Potash Farm," home of Rush the murderer. Portraits of famous highwaymen on horseback are more understandable; they have a romantic appeal.

Biblical and religious subjects offer a fertile field. From time to time we come across an anti-clerical twist, for instance, a group of a farmer and his wife offering the parson their tenth child. No survey, however cursory, of these Staffordshire figures could omit the immense field of sport. Here is a whole gallery of bygone champions, from Tom Cribb the boxer to the famous horse Eclipse. Bull-baiting, bear-baiting and the many field sports are all abundantly represented. Conviviality too fills a large place, whilst drunkenness, then as now, was an endless source of amusement. Nor must we forget the stage. Many of the favourites of the tinsel picture make a simultaneous appearance in earthenware, with the same heroic stance and vivid colour schemes.

Then there are idyllic cottages, churches, castles; they reflect the romantic and picturesque fashion then prevalent in architecture, the toy Gothic of St. John's Wood; and again, the castles are of the same shapes as those still painted on canal barges.

Such are some of the many subjects covered by these image toys. Perhaps the most attractive are those which record nothing special; the multitude of animals and birds, many with oddly human and sentimental expressions, cows, sheep, dogs spotted or plain, cats and little human personages. Often these little figures hit off perfectly some characteristic of their subject, although the representation makes small attempt at literal portrayal.

The idea of making vessels in grotesque human or animal shape must be one of the oldest of potters' jokes. In England "Bellarmine" stoneware bottles with a face on them were known long before they got their name from an unpopular Cardinal. One of the offshoots of the Bellarmine joke is the Toby Jug. Others are the stoneware or earthenware flasks and bottles, ancestors of our present ginger-beer bottles, which were produced in all sorts of grotesque forms.

The Mermaid, made at Rockingham, earthenware glazed a rich chocolate brown like the well-known teapots, is evidently intended to lie in a basket, as her scaly tail curves round so much that she cannot be stood upright; she is to be found with several different faces, but invariably extremely *décolletée*. The Toper is an old gentleman astride a barrel, holding a glass in either hand; his top-hat holds the cork.

The stoneware bottles, made, most of them, at Lambeth, Fulham and Denby, are a much lighter brown, ranging sometimes to yellow ochre, and the details come out more incisively. The Lambeth fish is very handsome; he measures some $11\frac{1}{2}$ inches; he holds the cork in his mouth, and he too cannot be stood upright. There is a flask shaped like a policeman's truncheon to commemorate Sir Robert Peel's introduction of the new police force in 1829. Another is made like an old-fashioned horse pistol, such as travellers habitually carried against highwaymen. Another is the size and shape of a big potato, one of the raw materials of whisky, but also said to have been used for smuggling spirits in a basket of vegetables into the hated new workhouses where alcohol was forbidden. Books, barrels, a railway clock, are some of the other shapes.

The Reform Bill controversy produced a great crop of portrait flasks, half-length representations of the King and the Whig leaders, suitably inscribed—"William IV's Reform Cordial," "The True Spirit of Reform." Rather incongruously the young Queen Victoria features as a full-length flask; wearing her crown and evening dress, she carries a scroll inscribed "My Trust is in My People." More flattering likenesses are obtained in the portrait medallions struck on the sides of square bottles.

During the early nineteen-hundreds an attempt was made to revive these portrait flasks, but the new are nothing like as successful as the old; the modelling seems too careful; it lacks the old dash, vigour and unself-consciousness.

Transfer printing offers an excellent means of pottery decoration, easily multiplied, yet dependent for its effectiveness on the individual quality of the engraving, done by hand, so that mass production need not necessarily mean a decline in aesthetic standards. It is not surprising to find that transfer printing has been successfully adapted to the needs of popular art.

So great, indeed, is the variety, that we can only arbitrarily draw attention to a few examples.

In a seafaring country, where families are often parted, mementoes are much in demand. By transfer printing, pieces can be suitably inscribed and decorated at small cost. Some of the most attractive souvenir pieces are the Newcastle and Sunderland pink lustre motto pottery which flourished from about the 1780's till well on into the nineteenth century. They are roughly decorated with untidy waves and marblings of pink lustre round the rims and framing the white panels on the front and sides, in which the pictures or verses are transfer printed. The print is decorated overglaze with splashes of vivid colour, red, green and yellow, making little attempt to keep within the outline. Perhaps it is this very feeling of freedom, combined with an extraordinarily sure sense of colour, that gives these things their charm.

One of the subjects most commonly illustrated on the largest jugs, bowls or mugs is the iron bridge across the Wear opened in 1796, no mean engineering feat for those days, and a source of local pride. The Sailor's Return and the Sailor's Farewell very often appear with appropriate verses, as do ships and nautical gear; sometimes a punch-bowl would be specially made to commemorate the sailing of some ship. Masonic emblems, arranged rather haphazardly, form with their cryptic verses pleasantly inconsequential designs for the uninitiated. There are also agricultural motives and some very dashing sporting jugs, sometimes with raised designs.

Smaller pieces generally have pink lustre banding. Sometimes the picture itself is not transferred but roughly hand-painted in lustre, rather like a child's drawing. The plate illustrated belongs to the anti-Corn-Law struggle of the 'forties. The wheatsheaf and agricultural implements are framed in roses, thistles and shamrocks, as befits a national campaign.

Besides political there is also religious instruction. Faith, Hope and Charity appear very charmingly on tea services. More forbidding are the text plaques to be hung up on the walls and bearing in bold letters an admonitory text.

Imaginary arms of various trades, sailor's, farmer's, mason's, were used as transfer decoration by all the big pottery centres, Staffordshire, Liverpool, Leeds, Sunderland, Newcastle and the rest, the idea being presumably derived from inn signs. The opening of the railways produced a crop of railway pieces, with pictures of the Rocket and other famous railway events. Indeed, the history of the early British railways can be traced in these simple wares, and the old patterns may still sometimes be found on new products, though they have lost some of the pleasant quality of the old, through over-careless production.

Election campaigns were excellent opportunities for transfer printing to provide a reasonably good, if rather crude, likeness of the candidate, suitably inscribed. Popular heroes and great events, coronations, victories, supplied other themes. As the nineteenth century advanced the process of porcelain

ENGRAVED GLASS FROM "YE OLDE SWAN," NOTTING HILL GATE, LONDON

making was cheapened, and so we find the increasingly popular "Presents from places" made in cheap china, but with the old decorative tradition persisting. Unfortunately, the decline in taste coincided with the introduction of cheap coloured lithographs for transfers from abroad, and it is this method which has made some of the worst modern atrocities possible.

A joke often found in the old Sunderland lustre and other contemporary mugs is a model of a toad or lizard put at the bottom to give the drinker a fright. Another "surprise" mug is so designed that, when tilted, its contents disappear into the handles, which are hollow. Some of the old inscriptions, too, are curiously discouraging. One runs:

> "Women make men love, and love makes them sad.
> Sadness makes them drink, and drink drives them mad."

As glass is so fragile, examples of popular art in it have rarely survived except for medieval stained glass, which hardly falls within our scope.

Lustred glass and earthenware were used as cheap substitutes for silver, but, as often happens, they soon ceased to be a crude imitation and developed individual qualities. At one time churches in the poorer parishes used altar vessels of silvered earthenware or glass, which proved very attractive for secular use also—vases, candlesticks and other ornaments, gaily painted on the outside with bright bands of colour and groups of flowers. They were used as prizes in the side-shows of fairs on account of their glitter and cheapness. Glass Christmas tree ornaments, birds with spun-glass tails, little coloured balls and other shapes, are too well known to require description; modern ones are usually imported from the Continent.

Some of these glass objects played a special part in country superstitions. Glass balls of varying sizes, silvered and daubed with patches of bright colour, used to be made, amongst other places, at Nailsea, for cottagers to hang in the window against the evil eye. As late as the 1840's, cottagers in Devonshire are described as setting up rods and crooks of twisted glass as a cure for fevers.

Like pottery, glass has been much used for love-tokens. Sailors and soldiers often gave a glass rolling-pin, hollow in the middle, with flowers and appropriate inscriptions painted on the outside, or sometimes a ship, flags, or well-known landmark.

Glass can be worked into all sorts of fantastic shapes, giving great scope to individual skill. Many of the amusing and intricate little ornaments we associate with, say, Nailsea—miniature coach horns which blow a note, bells, bellows, even pipes—were *tours de force* made by individual glass workers.

The Nailsea Glass Workers' Guild even made their own pole-head emblems of blown *latticinio* glass. The elaborate glass fountain, with coloured birds perching amongst a fantastic pyramid of twisting arches, to be seen in the Victoria and Albert Museum, is a remarkable example both of skill and of a sense of beautifully balanced form and colour. Foreign workmen, Venetians and French, introduced many of the decorative techniques to England, but these foreign strains have become pleasantly assimilated to native talents.

During the nineteenth century there developed another form of popular art in glass, the engraved glass screen or window, which now mainly survives in public-houses. Engraved (or "brilliant") glass sparkles but also obscures the view; it thus suited the strong urge for privacy, particularly associated with drinking, which prevailed in nineteenth-century England, whilst helping to create a festive atmosphere, one of the attractions of old-fashioned public-houses to survive long after the bad old days of glittering gin palaces and "drunk for a penny, dead drunk for twopence," though it is now gradually giving way before the new social trends represented in the modern "road-house."

Many of these engraved glass screens have elaborate and very decorative designs of scrolls, festoons, fruit and flowers. Sometimes the sign of the public-house is introduced, a swan, perhaps, or a ship. Often the lower half of the glass panel is frosted and the upper left clear, which throws up the design against contrasting textures. For wall decorations, engraved mirrors are used with the same style of patterns; in pairs these mirrors reflect each other with an enchanting effect of spaciousness and brilliancy. Engraved mirrors were once much used for theatres, shops and other display centres. They may still sometimes be seen in old-fashioned grocers' shops, engraved with pictures of the various spice plants, nutmeg or cocoa; alongside the painted tea tins and jars, they suggest an Oriental abundance.

The decorative motives used in this engraved glass derive from the early

Victorian hotchpotch of styles which reached its zenith at the Great Exhibition of 1851. A tangle of conventionalised twists and twirls, rococo and pseudo-Gothic, combine with extremely naturalistic fruits and flowers. As the century progresses, the curves begin to lose their spring, the patterns grow more stereotyped, the Gothic motives more obtrusive; they lose their playful picturesque qualities, become pinched and stiff, and take on a machine-made look; not that they are machine-made, but because gaiety and spontaneity are lost as the Gothic Revival ousts the Romantic Movement.

BONE STAYBUSK AND CARVED WOODEN ROLLER
Pencil drawings by Enid Marx

PAINTING, CARVING AND METALWORK

CARVING is comparatively durable. We can trace a long tradition of popular art in it, ranging from the early Christian era of the great stone Northumbrian crosses, or even from pre-Christian times if we include the White Horses or Cerne Abbas giant cut out in the chalk of the Downs, on through the wealth of medieval and renaissance carvings to the ships' figureheads and roundabout horses of the nineteenth century. With such an abundance, we can only pick a few examples.

The figurehead is one of the most characteristic forms of wood carving in England, and has lasted from Tudor times, when sailing-ships developed a beak, right down to the beginning of this century, when iron replaced wood for shipbuilding. In its heyday, the carving ran right round the ship to finish in a blaze of magnificence at the stern. The changes in style and type of the "carved works" on English ships, together with the long struggle between the sailors who insisted on them and the economising tendencies of the Admiralty, may be studied in Mr. L. G. Carr Loughton's *Old Ships' Figureheads and Sterns.*

We can no longer see figureheads placed as their carvers meant, but they may often be found, set up in seaports or as inn signs, as well as in special collections like that of the Royal Maritime Museum, Greenwich.

31

FIGUREHEAD OF H.M.S. CENTURION

In the West Country, figureheads of lost ships might be set up as a memorial to the crew, as in Morwenstow churchyard or Bude, whilst a great many are to be found in the Scilly Isles, a grim reminder of past wrecks.

Few of these surviving figureheads are earlier than the nineteenth century, by when single figures of simple design were common, especially on naval vessels; they grew in size, till by the 1850's a three-quarter length figure might be fifteen feet high. With the arrival of the clipper, the position of the figure inclined more to the horizontal, which, together with the graceful lines of these fast sailing-ships, again affected their design. The vogue for realism led to portraits of royal personages or popular heroes. An attractive example is the fifteen-foot figurehead of the *Royal Albert*, dating from 1854, and now at Chatham. The Prince Consort, complete with side-whiskers, looks surprisingly like his little Staffordshire figure portraits. The many Oriental figures recall British interests in the East Indies. Portrait figureheads on merchantmen named after their owners sometimes give strange results; the *James Bains* is carved buttoned up in a frock coat; the *Samuel Plimsoll* actually had a top-hat. We can get some idea of the great variety, both in size and subject, if we recall that these nineteenth-century figureheads were carried by vessels of all sorts and conditions, from the man-o'-war and elegant clipper to the humble paddle-steamer.

32

BARGE DECORATION

Painted by Mr. Frank Jones of Leighton Buzzard, 1945

INN SIGN—KNIGHTS OF ST. JOHN TAVERN, C. 1820
Detail from a water colour sketch by Enid Marx
By courtesy of The Pilgrim Trust

What the figurehead was to the ship, the sign once was to the shop or inn. At a time when few could read, all shops displayed their signs, pictures or effigies or both. Shop signs are now comparatively rare, but most inns maintain them though sometimes in sadly degenerate form.

Signs may be painted on wood, carved in wood or stone, moulded in plaster or fashioned in metal. Mostly they were produced by local craftsmen, though during the late eighteenth and early nineteenth centuries, signmaking was a recognised industry. The subjects of signs, with some famous exceptions in the case of inns (usually derived from local corruptions of an older name) keep to a pretty definite range, though local design and execution often show much variety. There are historic, heraldic, religious and classical motives, emblems of various trades and professions, and, amongst inns especially, sporting motives, jokes and puns, commemorative and geographical subjects.

Few inn or other signs, in whatever material, survive from earlier than the late seventeenth century, though the stone carved and gilt angel's head bracket above the doorway of the Angel and Royal inn at Grantham is much older. Effigy signs, carved in the round, are usually placed over porticos, but sometimes, like the magnificent White Hart sign at Salisbury, on the gable of the roof. They are often

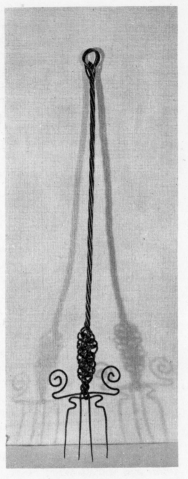

TWISTED WIRE FORK

beautifully carved with an economy and vigour admirably suited to their purpose. Plaques, carved or moulded in relief, are often set over doorways, for instance the painted plaster Knights of St. John illustrated here, which dates from the 1820's. Signboards are sometimes hung from a bracket, set up on a post or, in the old "gallows" form of a sign, of which a few examples still survive, slung from an archway across the road. These archways were often surmounted by figures such as the Four Swans at Waltham Cross.

The wrought-iron brackets or frames are often admirable examples of the work of local smiths. Sometimes they repeat in metal the device painted on the board, as in the famous Three Swans bracket at Market Harborough

33

PEARLIE KING

which dates from about 1700. Abstract scroll-work decoration is more common, sometimes ending in a bunch of grapes. Signboards on posts sometimes have decorative ironwork hoods, like The Bear at Woodstock; sometimes scroll-work frames. Indeed it is surprising how much variety can be put into the simple purpose of hanging up a board.

Much of this ironwork dates from the eighteenth century, but the signboards themselves have usually been frequently repainted owing to the effect of the weather, though the old device has sometimes been preserved. There are a few instances of signs painted by famous artists, Morland, Hogarth, Wilson and so on, but by far the great majority were local work. Examples of work in the same tradition but better preserved may often be seen as decoration in country churches; boards displaying the royal coat of arms, or with symbols of mortality, like the one here illustrated.

Another form of sign which displays the work of local craftsmen is the weathercock or weather-vane. Weathercocks are peculiarly English and were in use before the Norman conquest, as the Bayeux tapestry shows. The weather-vane, properly so-called, derives from the general medieval custom of using pennants or "fanes"; it often has an armorial or other device pierced in it. Interest in wind and weather is understandable in a seafaring country, as witness the wealth and variety of weather-vanes in London, especially on the City churches, before the air-raids. The cock illustrated has his wings, comb and wattles fitted on separately, to show up better from the ground, and tail set at an angle to catch the wind. Cocks are the most frequent, though from time to time we find other symbols, generally of local significance, like the gilded wooden fish on Charmouth church. The little Devonshire village of Spreyton formerly had, over the forge, the figure of a blacksmith hammering on an anvil; it had been most ingeniously made by the smith himself to work in the wind.

To the ingenuity of the country smiths and wheelwrights we also owe one of the latest and most flamboyant manifestations of popular carving and painting (the more remarkable because it arose as part of the industrial revolution), the elaborately carved and decorated roundabouts and swings of the fair-ground. The idea of grotesque figures at popular entertainments is immemorially old. The London Guildhall giants, Gog and Magog (alas,

34

FAIR-GROUND HORSE FROM A ROUNDABOUT AT KEW BRIDGE, LONDON

burnt in the blitz) were originally Lord Mayor's Show effigies, replacing those lost in an earlier conflagration. The hobby-horses of folk-dancing and mumming, once widespread, now survive only in a few country districts. Hobby-horses as children's toys evolved into the often beautifully carved rocking-horses of the eighteenth and nineteenth centuries, as also into the primitive merry-go-rounds with wooden horses on a revolving platform propelled by hand, which were the only entertainment of their kind some seventy years ago. The steam engine revolutionised the fair-ground rides as it did so much else. Most of the credit for applying steam to fair-ground entertainment goes to Frederick Savage, a country blacksmith and wheel-wright of King's Lynn, in Norfolk, where his statue stands to-day, though it must be confessed more for his achievements in developing agricultural machinery.

The extraordinarily elaborate decoration of roundabouts is the more remarkable if we remember that they have to be constantly transported;

35

everything must take to pieces quickly and easily. A steam engine in the middle drives a revolving centre, from which project steel shafts like the spokes of a wheel, to carry horses and platform. Every possible bit of space is flamboyantly decorated. The revolving centre is enclosed by sets of carved and painted panels; at the top these are crowned with elegant scroll-work carving and edged with scalloped or lozenge "droppers," each carved and painted, often with an engraved "brilliant" mirror inset. The curved, or "rounding," boards forming the rim of the wheel are similarly orna-mented, and bear the owner's name in lettering elaborately twirled, shaded and picked out in colours. Where joins occur, as they frequently must, bits of carving hide them.

Such is the background for the horses. Hung four or five abreast from shiny twisted brass rods (nowadays mostly chromium) the outermost "galloper" is usually elaborately carved and painted; the decoration grows progressively less and the innermost one may be painted only. Naturalism is at a discount. Not only harness and trappings, but the whole body of the horse may be patterned with handsome scallops and scrolls, acanthus leaf motives, or roses, thistles and shamrocks perhaps, with portrait medallions or grotesque masks on the flanks. Varnished paint, with details picked out in contrasting colours, heightens the effect. Individual gallopers vary very much; all adopt the traditional flying stance, but they have different decora-tions, as also different expressions. Each horse has his name inscribed on a ribbon round his neck. The rise of ostrich farming in South Africa, which supplied the costermonger's "Donah" with her traditional feathered hat, also suggested rideable birds to the showman. Ostriches took their

MEMENTO MORI. PAINTING ON WOOD IN LYME REGIS PARISH CHURCH
Pencil and wash drawing by Enid Marx

places alongside the horses, and in due course other birds also, turkeys, cockerels, peacocks, and sometimes hybrid creations, with the tail of one and the head of another. The birds mostly have a fierce grotesqueness reminiscent of Tibetan devil-masks, whilst scaly dragons look rather Chinese. The Switchback, cars revolving on an undulating platform, came rather later than the gallopers. The cars—gondolas, dragons and so on—gave less scope for variety in decoration, but the stationary platform is mounted by a magnificent flight of steps with ornamental balustrades, which might have come straight out of a Juvenile Drama palace.

As to the origins of all this decorative exuberance, the bones, as it were, obviously derive from the romanticised rococo of early nineteenth-century theatre decoration, as we may still see it in the Toy Theatre sets. Super-imposed on this we find the same inconsequential hotchpotch of styles and underlying sense of the magnificent that characterises the Great Exhibition of 1851. But what is so surprising is the way the old decorative tradition has persisted, assimilating, without undue incongruity, later ideas and motives, widely separated from each other in both space and time. You may find, for instance, a plaque of the head of some Boer War hero, in wide-brimmed hat, alongside a classical mask or an eighteenth-century stylised Britannia. The paintings on the panels, depicting, as they frequently do, the high spot of some terrific adventure, a tiger hunt perhaps, are lineal descendants of the old Raree or Peepshow. They continue the old, simple-minded homely style, whereby tigers take on the appearance of outsize domestic cats. Here and there more peaceful moods prevail; moonlit rocks and waterfall echo the romantic landscape of the Toy Theatre and the castles painted on barges.

In spite of exotic forms, this decoration remains characteristically English, as may often be seen by comparing it with the style of the richly ornate front of the steam organ, with its dancing automatons, which is usually of foreign workmanship. This form of popular art reached its heyday about the 1900's. From about the 1920's a decline set in; taste changed towards a more mechanical and streamlined style; motor-cars and aeroplanes replaced the horses; portraits of film stars were not, as had been the case with earlier celebrities, assimilated to the rococo spirit of the whole; stereo-typed cinema standards began to drive out the much more individual and rich traditions of the music hall. At present the change is proceeding very rapidly, and the old-style decoration is not likely to survive many more years.

By contrast, the painting on English canal barges, which has much in common with fair-ground decoration, still persists in its traditional forms. Attempts to explain these forms in terms of the mystic symbolism attached to boat decoration in other parts of the world are not very convincing; good luck is traditionally associated with the symbols of playing-cards found in barge decoration, but any deeper significance seems doubtful.

The most striking motives are castles and flowers. The castles are set in a little scene on a river. No two pictures must be identical, consequently architectural details vary quite a bit. Nevertheless they all have a recognis-able affinity to a common ancestor both in style and colour—the roman-ticised, picturesque castle that we also find in the Toy Theatre sheets. Nor is this surprising if we remember that English canals were being built apace from the 1760's to about the 1830's, which coincides with the early romantic phase of the Gothic Revival when picturesque castles were all the rage. The canal folk, in the early days, were many of them of gipsy origin, which in

MINIATURE CAST-IRON FIREPLACE WITH GRATE, FENDER
AND FIRE-IRONS OF POLISHED BRASS

turn may account for the resemblance between the bright colours and highly polished brass fittings of canal barges and those of caravans and fair-ground decoration.

Much of the attraction of barge decoration is due to the style of painting, which is extremely free, in the true peasant tradition. Deep bottle green or vermilion is a favourite ground for sprays of roses in contrasting colours of red, pink and yellow, with darker shading. The painter puts in the body of the rose with a few deft brush sweeps, adding the shading whilst the paint is still wet, to get a melting quality. Multi-petalled daisies, yellow, pink, red or blue, with contrasting centres, are set off, as are the roses, by light green foliage, elaborately veined and shaded. The lettering of the owner's name and place of origin is full of curls and twirls and elaborately shadowed, like the lettering on old-fashioned farm carts and fair-ground entertainments, with little garlands of flowers filling in the spaces and corners.

Besides castles and flowers, a bright geometrical pattern of circles and diamonds, known as "Scotch plaid," is also used. Each pattern seems to

39

have its traditional place—the tiller bar, for instance, is banded in contrasting colours like a barber's pole, only wider. Inside the cabin, elaborate paint-work bird's-eye graining fills in the background. The equipment is also ornamented; blocks and stands for gang planks, stools, even the large galvanised fresh water-can and washing-bowl. The water-can often has the owner's name inscribed on a scroll. Everything possible is decorated— one boat painted by Mr. Frank Jones of Linslade, Leighton Buzzard, has as many as two hundred flowers.

Painted decoration of farm carts, which has much in common with barge painting, is, unfortunately, rapidly disappearing. The painting is done on the front and tailboard, and it used to consist of panels, back and front, bearing the owner's and maker's names in shaded lettering, with decorations of scrolls and curls. Costermonger's carts are also often very prettily picked out in colour, a practice which seems to continue.

SAILOR'S PIN-CUSHION

TEXTILES

QUILTING is an old traditional cottage industry in England and was at one time common all over the country, though nowadays it survives directly only in certain regions, Wales and the North, though, through the efforts of the Rural Industries Bureau, it is being resuscitated in areas where it had previously virtually died out. Although the quilter usually designs her own pattern, she is naturally influenced by local tradition, so that experts are often able to identify the place of origin of a quilt by certain regional differences. Thus Mrs. Elizabeth Hake (*English Quilting, Old and New*) who has specially concerned herself with West Country quilting,

PRINTED COTTON COMMEMORATIVE HANDKERCHIEF

which was very nearly extinct, suggests that geometrical patterns are particularly associated with Wales, rather formalistic floral ones with the North, and freer flowing floral decoration with the West Country, though of course there can be no hard and fast rule. The different types of centres might also perhaps be attributed to regional traditions, but the revival of interest in English quilting is so recent that the question of comparative designs has been little explored. Nowadays only wadded or padded quilts are still made, though some of the earlier ones, with raised corded designs, are very decorative. Close stitching is sometimes used to throw up certain parts of a design.

In looking at English quilts, what is perhaps most remarkable, besides the utilisation of space to best advantage, is the number of different ways in which a few basic motives—cable, shell, feather, intersecting circles or diamonds and so on—can be used. Floral motives seem to have been studied and adapted from life.

41

Closely allied to quilting, and often combined with it, is patchwork. Although she is using bits of old material, the patchwork-maker has great scope for her individual decorative sense, not only in the arrangement of colours and textures, but also in the varying shapes into which she cuts her patches.

Smocking was once worn by countrymen all over England, but has now died out. The principle, of making a raised pattern on textiles, is the same as quilting, though the designs and methods are different. They varied, not according to the localities, but according to the trade of the wearer, conventional symbols of which were embroidered on the front, the idea being, apparently, that at country hirings the farmer could recognise the qualifications he required—ploughman, shepherd, dairymaid and so on—though no doubt professional pride also played its part, as with other uniforms. Smocking, like quilting, shows a remarkable decorative sense. Another form of textile decoration is knitting, of which the most interesting living survival in England is perhaps the fisherman's jersey or guernsey as knitted on the Yorkshire coast. Here the design varies according to the village from which the wearer comes, allegedly so that in case of disaster bodies washed ashore could be readily identified, but again local pride is undoubtedly part of the explanation.

Quilting, smocking, knitting, are all crafts which survive, if at all, only tenuously from a glorious past. But there is one form of popular textile decoration which seems to have arisen spontaneously during the last forty-five years. This is the costermonger's pearlie suit, which is decorated with fantastic patterns in pearl buttons. The traditional coster costume of the 'eighties and 'nineties was a square-cut jacket, with velvet collar and pocket flaps, a waistcoat, and bell-bottomed trousers, with a brightly coloured scarf and a bowler hat. The buttons on the coat and waistcoat were the usual number but made of pearl, or sometimes glass: the celebrated "Road to Ruin" buttons were glass with, inset, the traditional symbols of wine, women and song—horse, dog, wineglass, woman's head, etc. The women wore bright velveteen dresses, coloured scarves, pearl button boots and the huge ostrich-feather hat. This special costume has now disappeared. In order to have some sort of a fancy-dress for collecting for their various hospital societies, costers took to decorating ordinary suits with patterns made of pearl buttons, inventing the designs themselves. At one time they even adopted a version of Wild West cowboy suits. Many of the "pearlie" patterns show a pleasantly fantastic sense of decoration and are extremely effective. The custom is one more example of the urge to create popular art whenever opportunities allow.

Soldiers and sailors had their own forms of textile decoration, rugs, and above all, large and elaborately tasselled pin-cushions, usually heart-shaped and decorated with buttons, beads and pin heads. They were made as a pastime and for presents. Indeed, pin-cushions provide some of the most

Closely allied to quilting, and often combined with it, is patchwork

PATCHWORK QUILT IN SILK, SATIN AND VELVET
Mid-nineteenth Century

interesting examples of popular taste, commemorative, political, or simply as a pretext for decorative exuberance.

Tattooing, though not exactly textile decoration, is so akin to it in motives and design that we cannot forbear to mention it here. As a practice it is very old and is found in many parts of the world. It seems to have been rediscovered by sailors and soldiers in the East, which would account for the prevalence of exotic Oriental motives, especially dragons, amongst the hearts, linked initials, flowers, butterflies, anchors and other homely symbols of luck, fidelity and affection which we find repeated over and over again in other forms of popular art.

Printing has also been applied to cheap textile decoration. The printed cotton handkerchiefs and scarves of the nineteenth century really belong more to street literature than to textiles, with their commemorative, sporting and political pictures. Even the ornaments for borders are often more reminiscent of typography than of textile traditions, although they sometimes combine both together.

CHILDREN'S PENNY TOYS
Nineteenth Century

MISCELLANEOUS HANDIWORK AND DECORATION

THE desire to give presents, especially love-tokens, has stimulated much popular art, often in the simplest materials. A bit of bone, for instance, might be shaped into a staybusk, in the days when women of all classes wore these formidable articles of dress, and be decorated with hearts, arrows, linked initials or other devices, scratched in outline and coloured. Apple-corers or cheese-tasters, with the same sort of patterning, use the knuckle for the handle. Whip or walking-stick handles in wood or bone, and many other small objects show much ingenuity and decorative sense in exploiting natural forms; indeed, a living branch might be carefully trained for years to grow the right shape for a special bit of carving. A *tour de*

PROFESSOR BURCHETT'S DESIGNS FOR TATTOOING

force was to cut a spoon and fork linked together by a wooden chain all from the same piece. Carved knitting sticks, butterpats for stamping butter, gingerbread rollers, tobacco pipes, are a few examples of simple materials skilfully used. Sailors have always been great adepts at this, and one of their favourite and most ingenious achievements is the fitting of a model ship into a bottle, by jointing it so that it will pull upright on threads fixed in the cork.

Apprentices, too, had special forms of handiwork. The shoemakers' apprentices are responsible for many of the little wooden shoe-shaped snuff-boxes, often exquisitely carved and decorated with minute brass studs in the soles; they are also made in beaten pewter. So careful is the workmanship that we can trace a whole century or more of changing fashions in shoes from them. Apprentices would also make little replicas in the actual materials of their trade, for practice and samples; many miniature pieces of furniture are their work. The little cast-iron fireplace here illustrated, complete with brass fender and fire irons, is one such, and also shows the decorative possibilities of cast iron, in which there is a long tradition. Earlier examples of it are the elaborately ornamented firebacks made in Sussex. The big iron-foundries carried on the tradition, so that we even find them casting chimney-piece ornaments in iron, as well as semi-utilitarian objects, grotesque door-stops, scrapers, and so on. Such things were

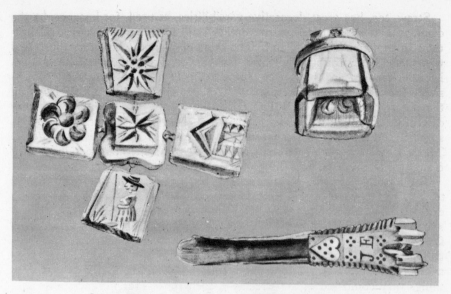

CARVED WOODEN BUTTER-PATS AND BONE APPLE-CORER

partially mass-produced, by contrast to the forged iron latches, hinges, fire-irons and innumerable other everyday objects where local smiths delighted to exercise their individual skill and pleasure in ornament.

The brasses or "medals" once worn by cart-horses on high days and holidays are another example of metal decoration. Originally pierced by hand from sheet metal, these brasses were at their best when cast in solid brass and polished, as they were till towards the end of the nineteenth century. The later phase of stamping them in brass detracts greatly from their appearance, although the traditional devices are preserved. Some of these devices, such as the crescent moon, the sun in various forms, and stars, are believed to be very old; others have been added from time to time; indeed, we often find topical allusions, such as a railway engine or even the portrait of a popular hero. Some of the same motives, crescents, stars, a hand, appear in the brass polehead emblems formerly carried in processions by local guilds and associations, which gave great scope for fantastic invention. The metal trade-tokens, once issued in lieu of small change by shops and inns, often preserve the old sign devices. A strange essay in the grotesque are the so-called "Billy and Charlie" fakes of the 1850's, when two illiterate workmen started making spurious medieval antiquities, medals and the like, and passing them off as discoveries during building excavations in London, thereby puzzling antiquarians not a little. The resultant hotch-potch of quasi-medieval motives, though without rhyme or reason, has surprising charm and vivacity.

Straw, too, has great decorative possibilities, as used, for instance, by the country thatcher. Plaited straw "dollies" still form part of harvest celebrations in some parts of England. The cross of plaited wheat-ears illustrated was made by a country labourer for harvest festival church decoration. More ephemeral are the flower posies still sold in country markets—Barnstaple for one. In the selection and arrangement of colours, they carry on the old traditional taste of the "florist's flowers" of a century ago, once carefully cultivated in cottage gardens for their bright contrasting stripes, speckles and lacings, as Mr. Jason Hill describes in *The Curious Gardener*. The artificial wreaths of white china flowers, still sometimes seen in country churchyards, preserve something of the same quality.

Toy-making, not the expensive kind, but penny toys for street hawkers to sell, had become a full-time family occupation by the mid-nineteenth century, and often produced delightful examples of popular art; this in spite of the miserable poverty of toy-makers, as the competition of imported foreign toys drove down wholesale prices. Jointed "Dutch" dolls, horses and carts, birdcages, soldiers, money boxes and much else besides were made in wood, in the traditional forms; children especially delighted in things they could see in the streets—garden rollers, for instance, were said to be less popular, since so few poor children had ever seen a real garden. Toys in tin and pewter, doll's house equipment and sets of toy soldiers were slightly more expensive. Early nineteenth-century toy soldiers, two-dimensional and gaily painted, often give scenes of camp life, like those here illustrated. The workmanship of the toys and other cheap objects sold by hawkers is often of a high level, as witness the penny toasting-fork here illustrated.

The attraction of souvenirs from places has also stimulated popular art, at first amateur, later professional. The use of sea shells for decorating boxes and frames, or of coloured sand for making patterns in glass weights, are but two examples which could be multiplied indefinitely.

MINIATURE TIN SOLDIERS, C. 1815

AUTHORS' NOTE AND SHORT BIBLIOGRAPHY

In spite of the many varied forms which English popular and traditional art has taken, surprisingly little has been written about it, at least in its more modern manifestations. A great deal has been written about medieval craftsmanship so that we have felt able to omit it from this brief survey. For the more modern forms, no general survey, such as has been made in most other countries, ever seems to have been attempted in England. Monographs have been devoted to certain aspects, such as pottery or chapbooks, and special articles may be found in periodicals such as *The Connoisseur, The Studio,* and *The Architectural* Review, though they generally tend to be written from the point of view of craftsmanship or rarity value. Only a few of our local museums have devoted special sections to popular art as such. The chief monographs used in the text are:

The Earthenware Collector, 1920, by G. Woolliscroft Rhead.—*English Pottery,* 1924, by B. Rackham and H. Read.—*London Tradesmen's Cards,* 1925, by Sir Ambrose Heal.—*Old Ships' Figureheads and Sterns,* 1925, by L. G. Carr Loughton.—*Children's Books in England,* 1932, by F. J. Harvey Darton.—*Penny Plain and Twopence Coloured,* 1932, by A. E. Wilson.—*English Quilting, Old and New,* 1937, by Elizabeth Hake.—*Silhouettes,* 1938, by Mrs. F. Nevill Jackson.—*English Smocks,* 1928, by Alice Armes

PLAITED STRAW DOLLIE
FOR HARVEST THANKSGIVING